KINGS & QUEENS OF COUNTRY SHEET MUSIC

The BIGGEST HITS from COUNTRY'S TOP ARTISTS
Arranged by Dan Coates

Alfred Publishing Co., Inc.
16320 Roscoe Blvd., Suite 100
P.O. Box 10003
Van Nuys, CA 91410-0003
alfred.com

Cover Photos
Lone Cowboy: © istockphoto / Cynthia Baldauf • Scrollwork: © istockphoto / Gintaras Svalbonas
Crown: © istockphoto / Roy Konitzer

ALL-AMERICAN GIRL

Words and Music by Carrie Underwood,
Kellie Lovelace and Ashley Gorley
Arranged by Dan Coates

Moderate country rock

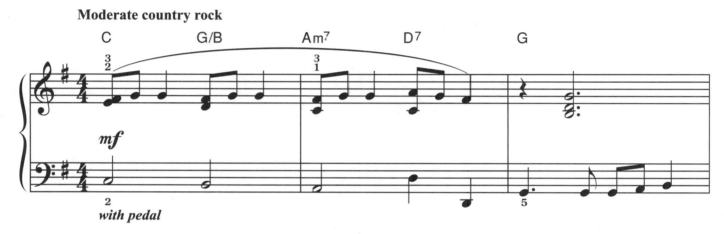

Verse:

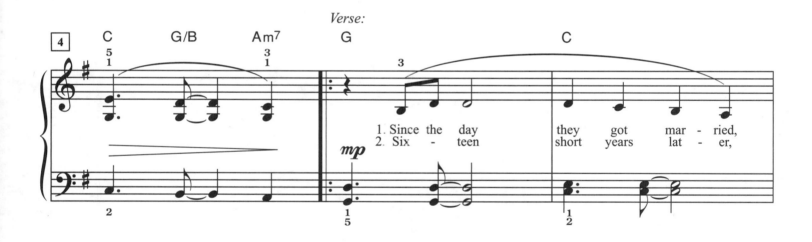

1. Since the day they got mar - ried,
2. Six - teen short years lat - er,

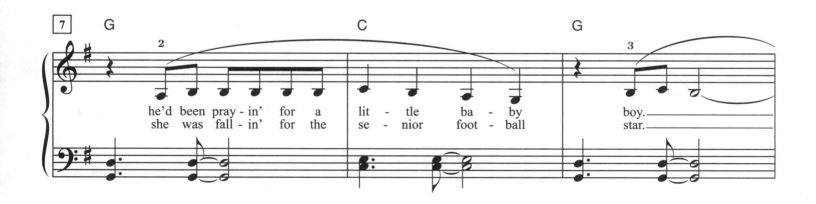

he'd been pray - in' for a lit - tle ba - by boy.
she was fall - in' for the se - nior foot - ball star.

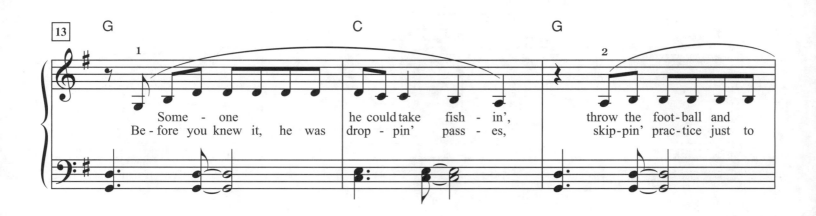

Some - one he could take fish - in',
Be - fore you knew it, he was drop - pin' pass - es,

throw the foot-ball and
skip-pin' prac-tice just to

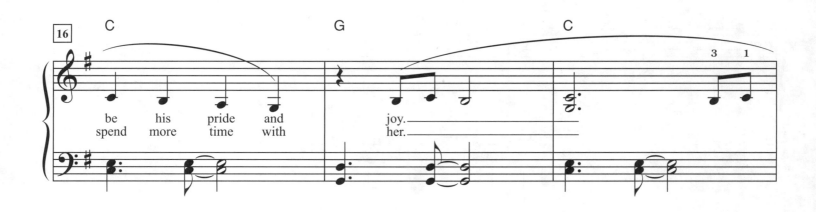

be his pride and
spend more time with

joy.
her.

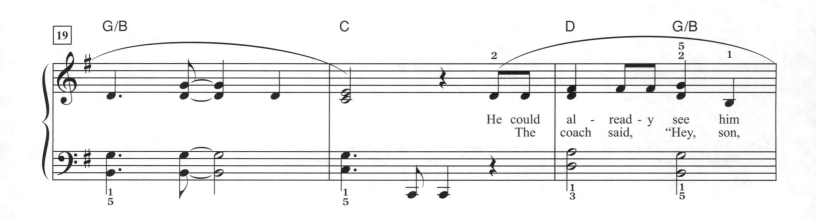

He could al - read - y see him
The coach said, "Hey, son,

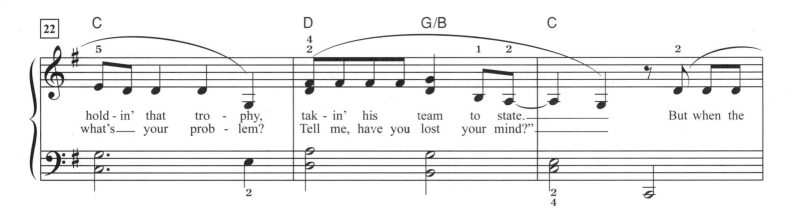

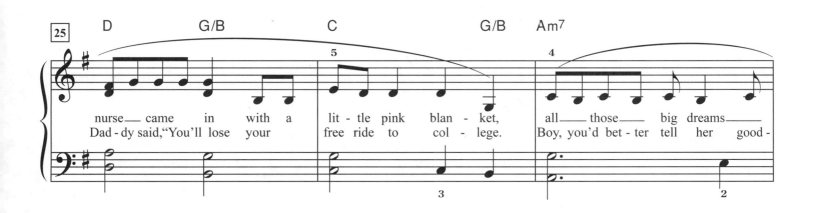

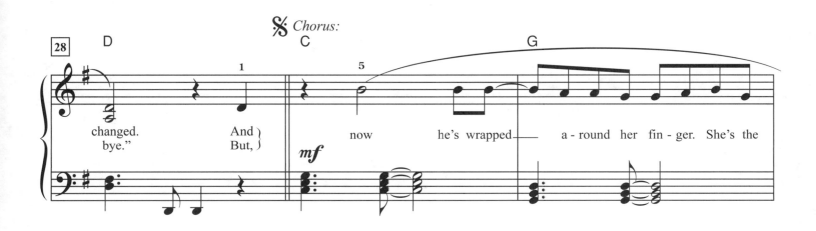

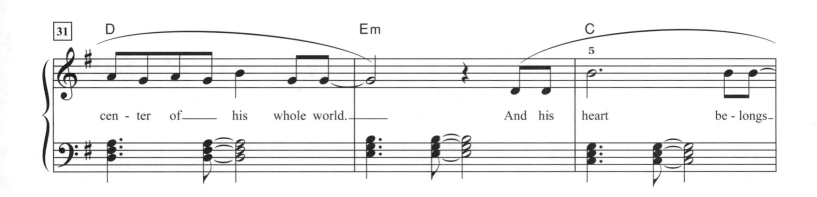

to Coda ⊕

to that sweet lit - tle, beau - ti - ful, won - der - ful, per - fect All - A - mer - i - can...

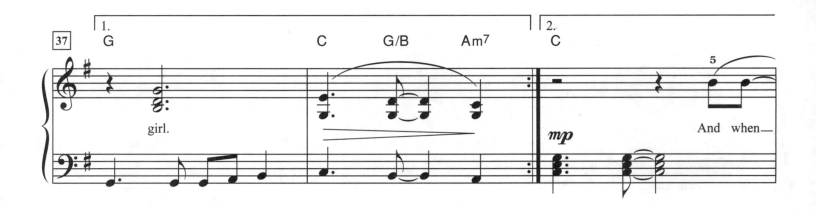

1.
girl.

2.
And when—

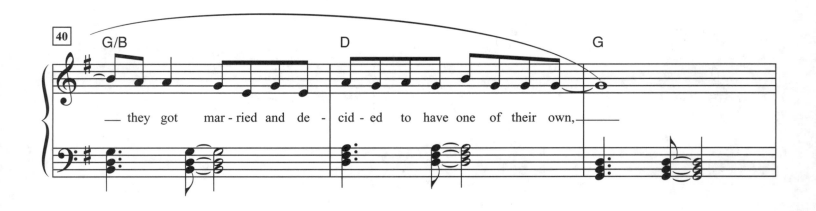

— they got mar - ried and de - cid - ed to have one of their own,—

she said, "Be hon - est, tell me what you want." And he said, "Hon - ey, you ought - a know,—

46

C   G/B   Am⁷   G/B

—   a   sweet   lit - tle, beau - ti - ful,   oh,   a

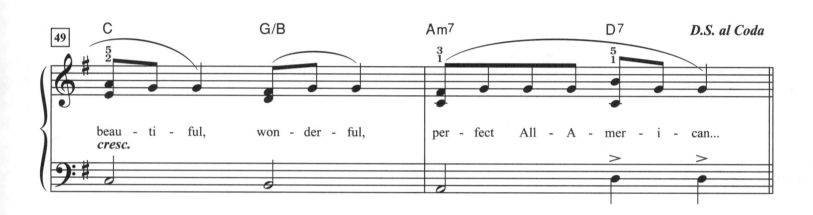

49

C   G/B   Am⁷   D⁷   *D.S. al Coda*

beau - ti - ful,   won - der - ful,   per - fect   All - A - mer - i - can...

cresc.

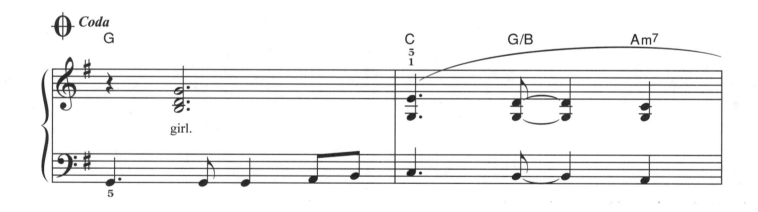

Coda
G   C   G/B   Am⁷

girl.

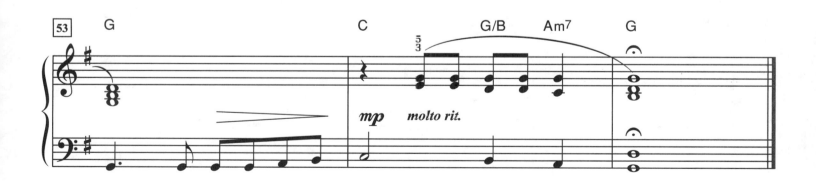

53

G   C   G/B   Am⁷   G

mp   *molto rit.*

THE DANCE

Words and Music by Tony Arata
Arranged by Dan Coates

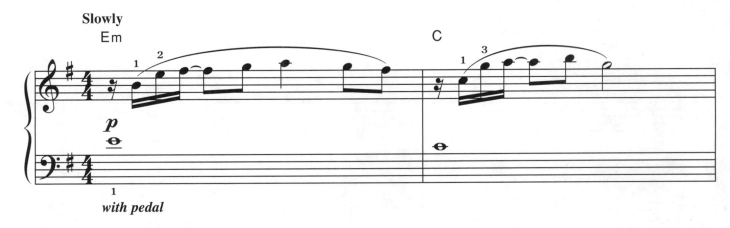

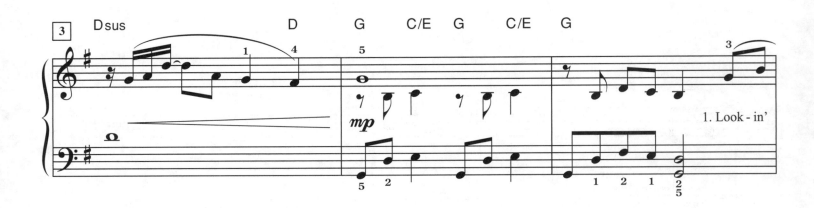

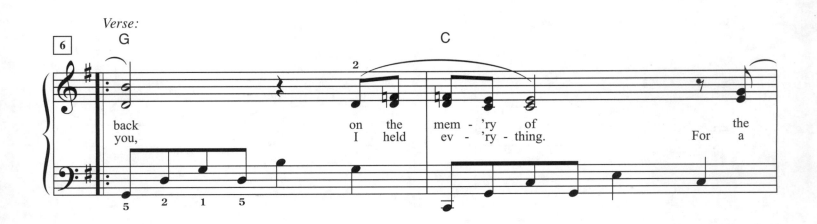

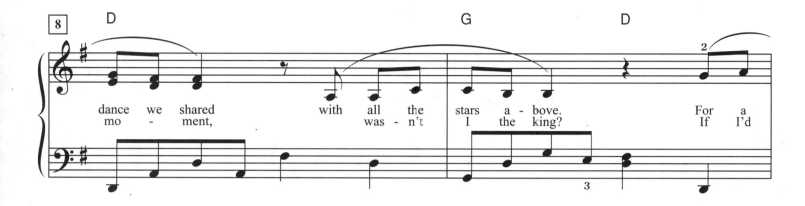

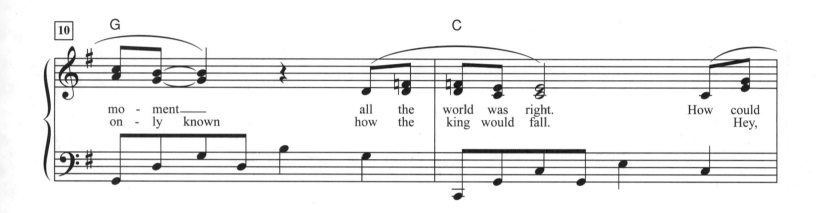

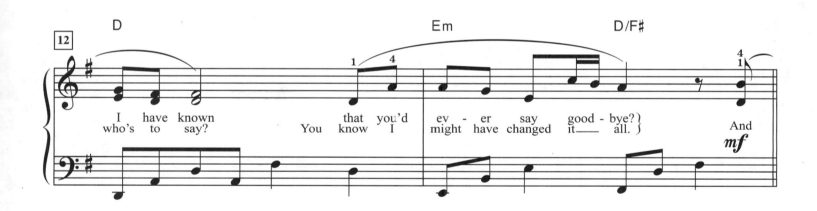

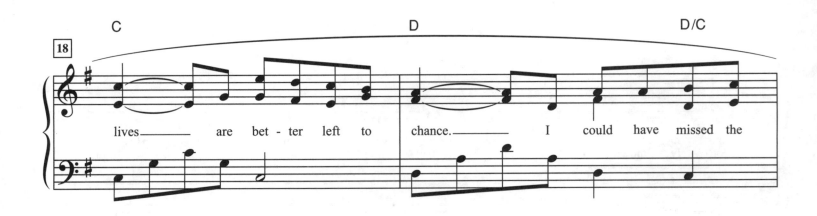

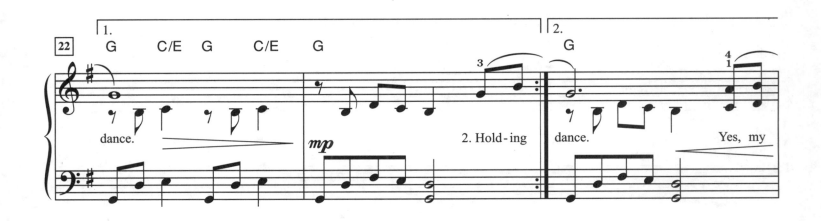

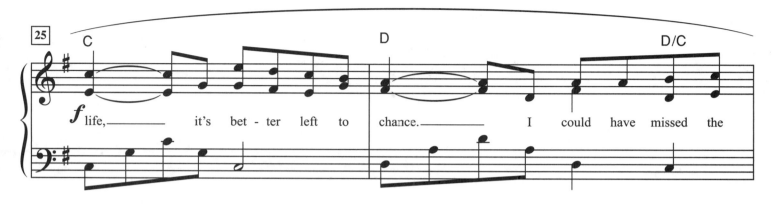

25
C　D　D/C

f life,_____ it's bet - ter left to　chance._____　I could have missed the

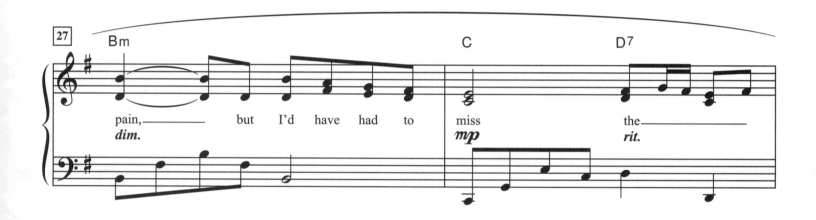

27
Bm　C　D⁷

pain,_____ but I'd have had to　miss　the_____

dim.　*mp*　*rit.*

29
a tempo
G　Em　C

dance.

p

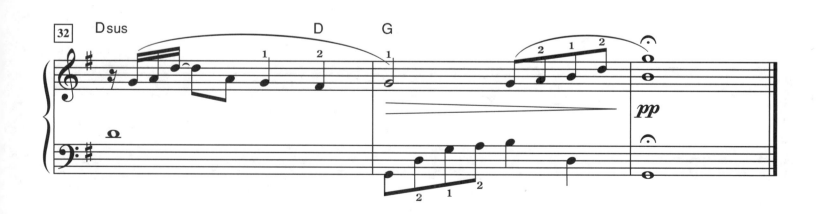

32
Dsus　D　G

pp

BECAUSE OF YOU

Words and Music by Kelly Clarkson,
Ben Moody and David Hodges
Arranged by Dan Coates

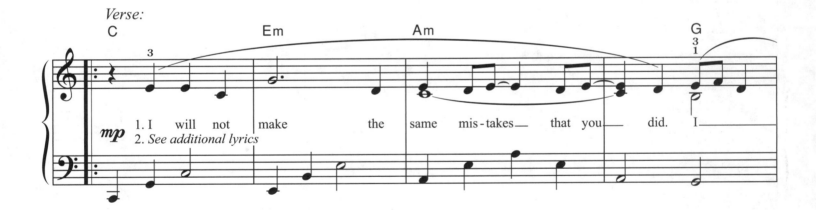

1. I will not make the same mis-takes that you did. I

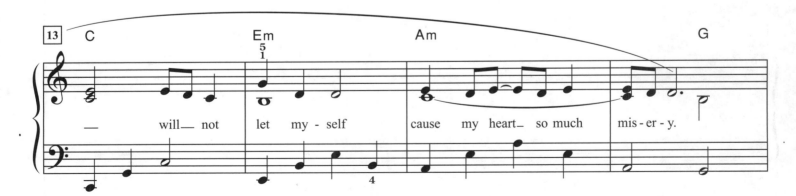

will not let my-self cause my heart so much mis-er-y.

Verse 2:
I lose my way,
And it's not too long before you point it out.
I cannot cry,
Because I know that's weakness in your eyes.
I'm forced to fake a smile,
A laugh, every day of my life.
My heart can't possibly break
When it wasn't even whole to start with.
(To Chorus:)

DON'T ROCK THE JUKEBOX

Words and Music by Alan Jackson,
Roger Murrah and Keith Stegall
Arranged by Dan Coates

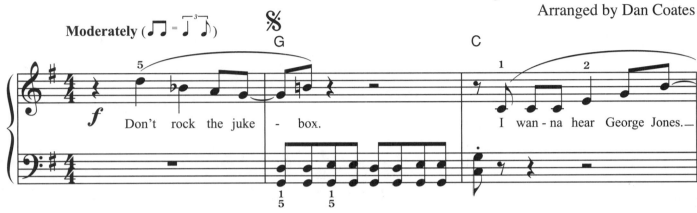

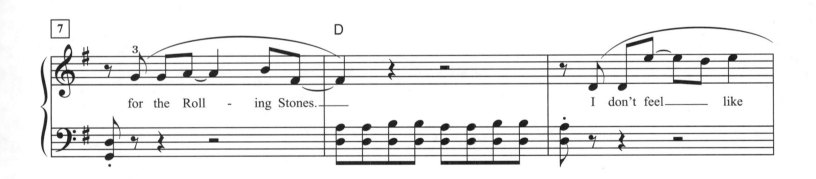

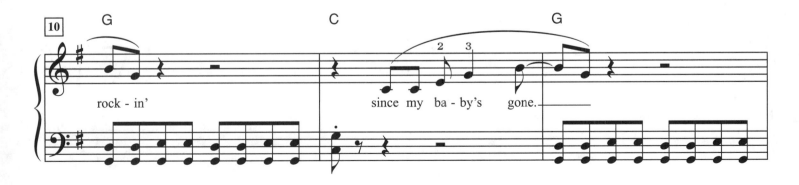

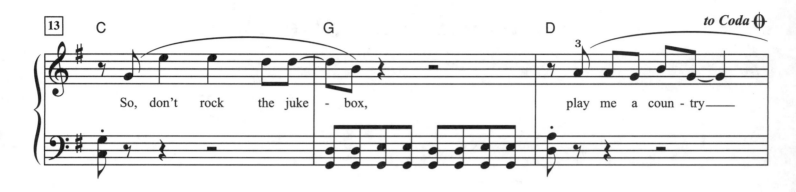

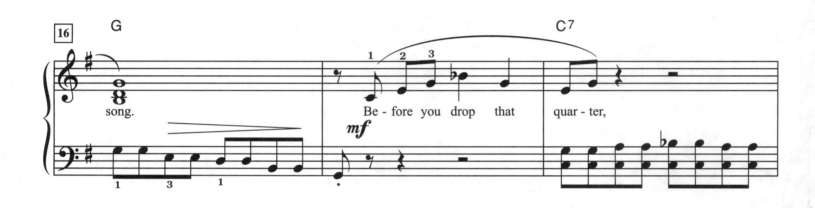

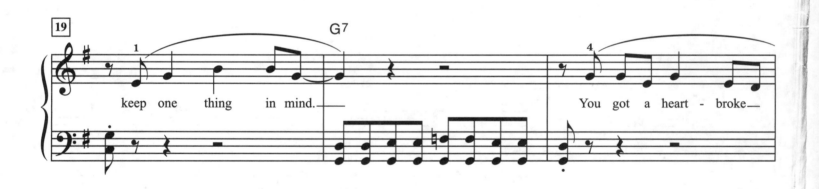

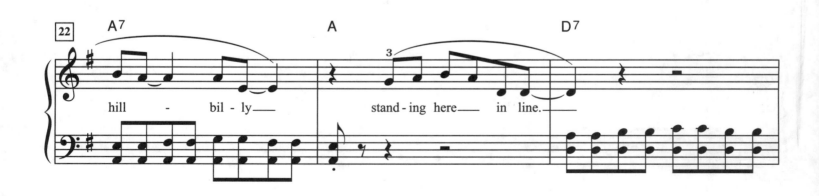

HOW DO I LIVE

Words and Music by Diane Warren
Arranged by Dan Coates

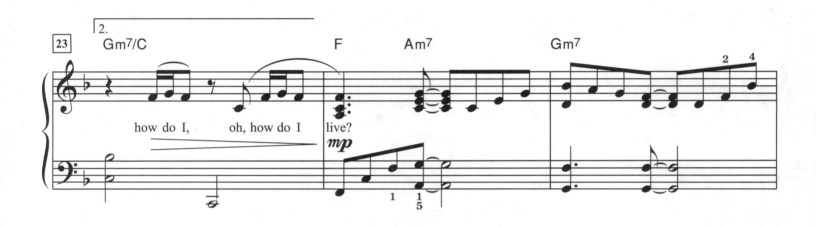

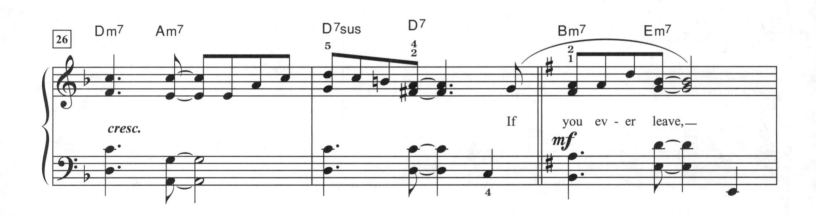

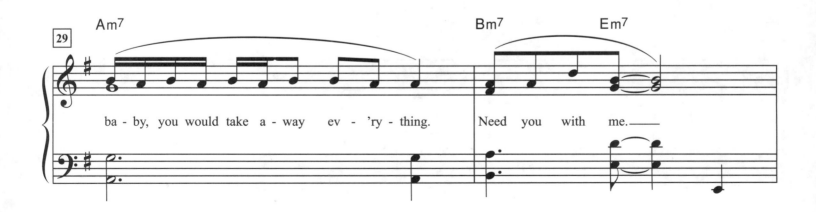

Verse 2:
Without you, there'd be no sun in my sky,
There would be no love in my life,
There'd be no world left for me.
And I, baby, I don't know what I would do,
I'd be lost if I lost you.
If you ever leave,
Baby, you would take away everything
Real in my life.
And tell me now...
(To Chorus):

I CROSS MY HEART

Words and Music by
Steve Dorff and Eric Kaz
Arranged by Dan Coates

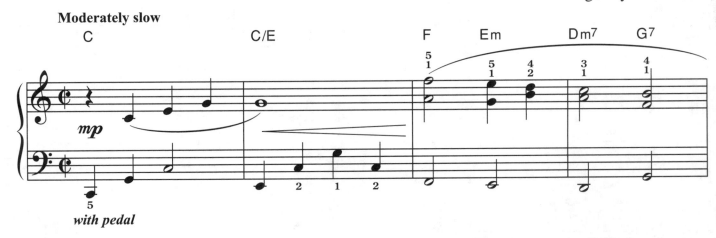

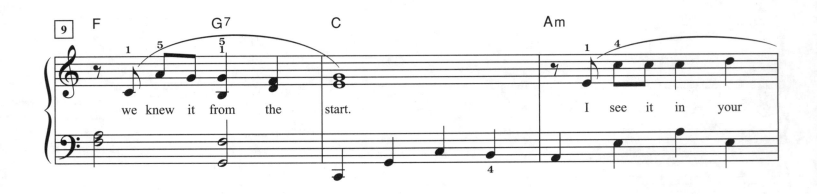

From here on af - ter,_____ let's stay the way we are_____ right_____

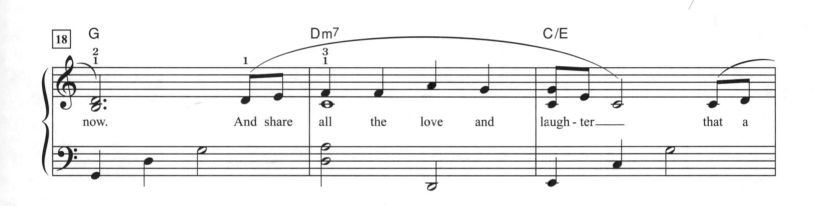

now. And share all the love and laugh - ter_____ that a

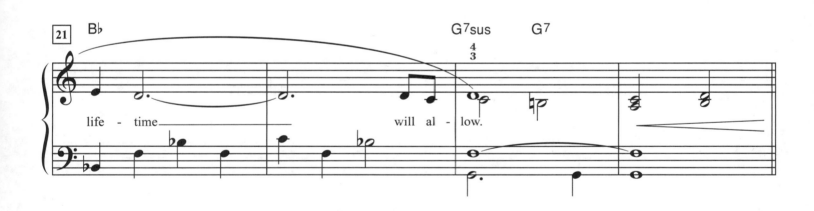

life - time_____ will al - low.

% *Chorus:*

I cross my heart and prom - ise to

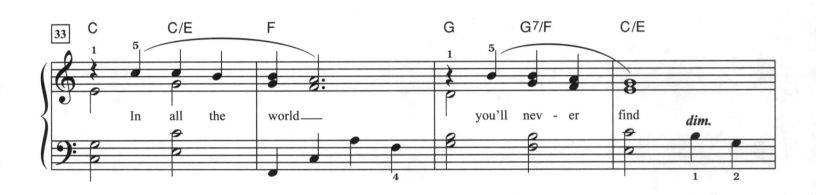

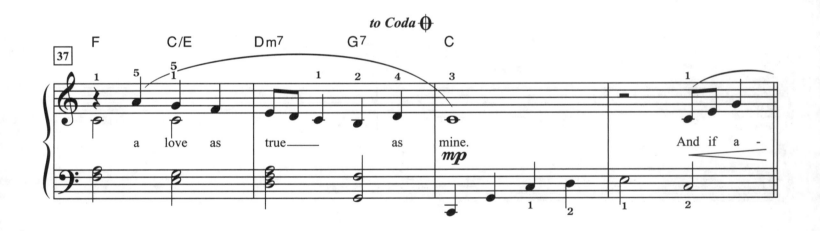

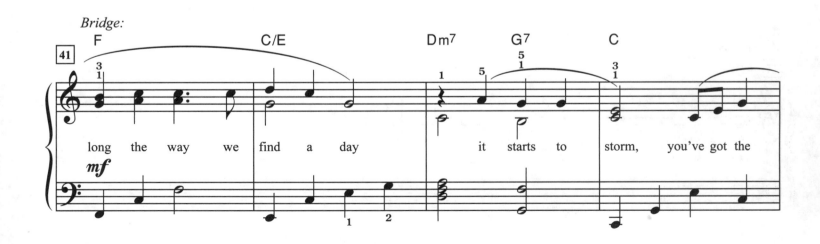

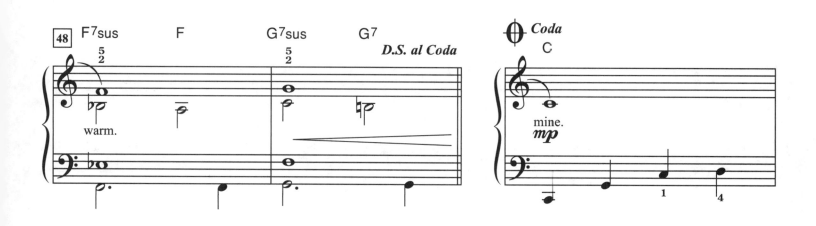

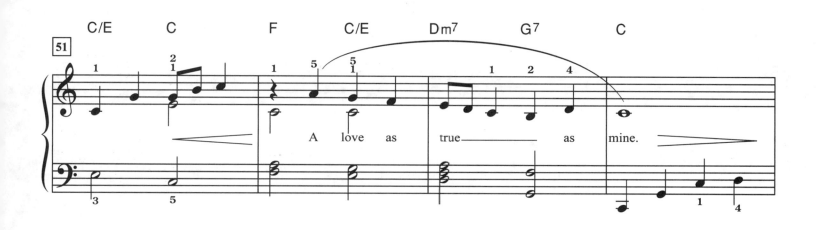

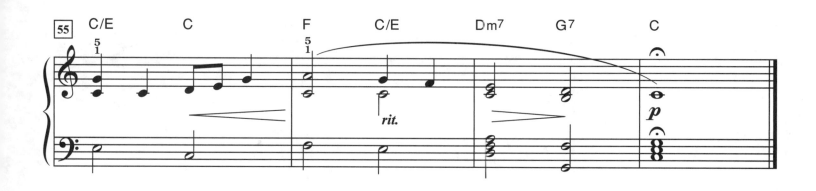

I SWEAR

Words and Music by
Gary Baker and Frank Myers
Arranged by Dan Coates

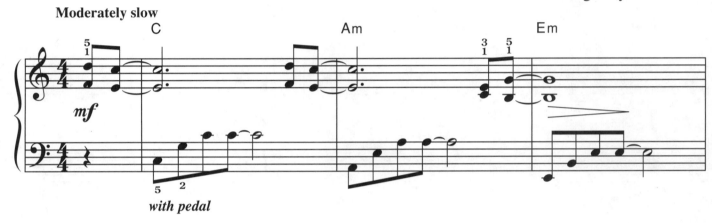

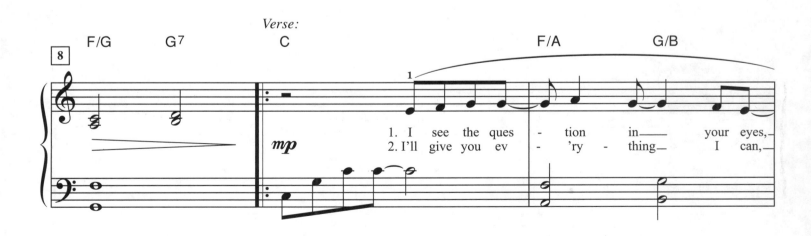

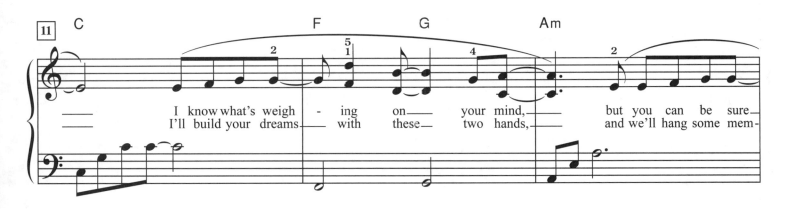

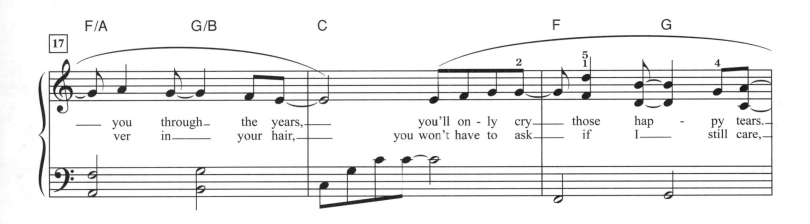

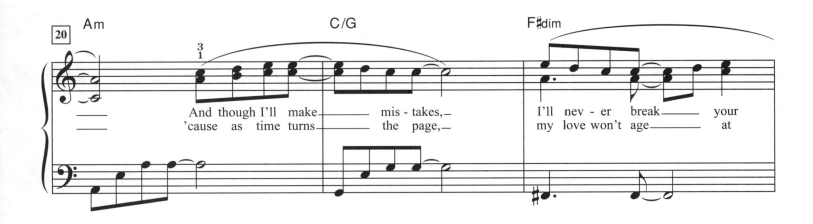

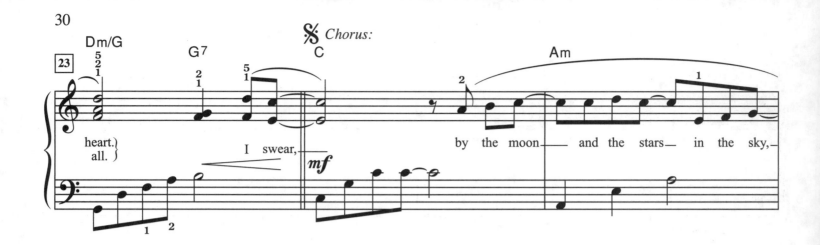

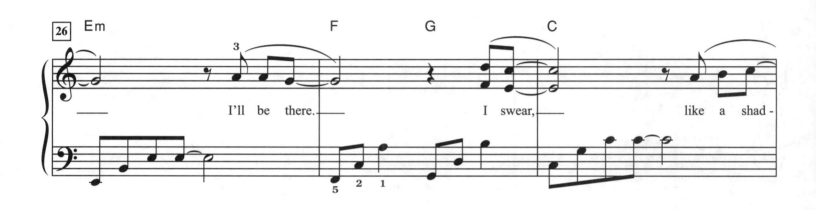

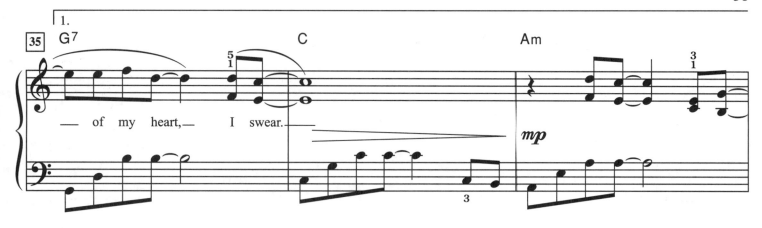

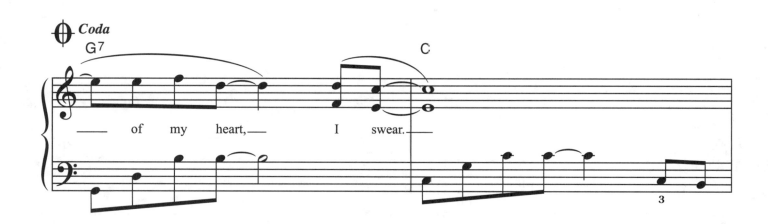

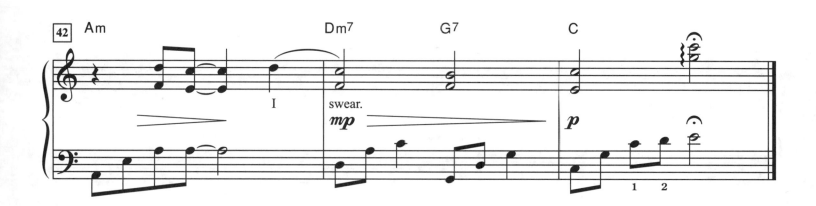

LIKE WE NEVER LOVED AT ALL

Words and Music by John Rich,
Vicky McGehee and Scott Sacks
Arranged by Dan Coates

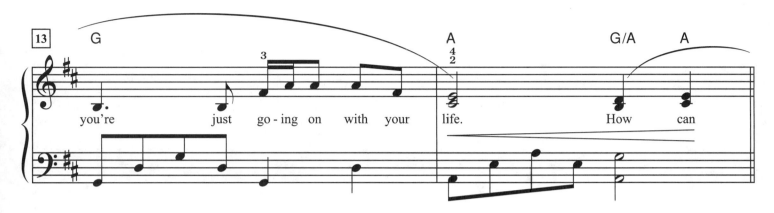

you're just go-ing on with your life. How can

Chorus:

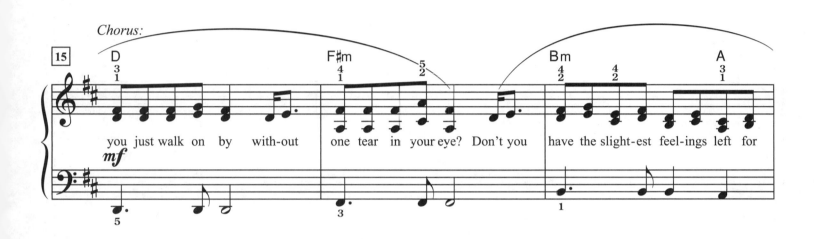

you just walk on by with-out one tear in your eye? Don't you have the slight-est feel-ings left for

me? May-be that's just your way of deal-ing with the pain, for-get-ting

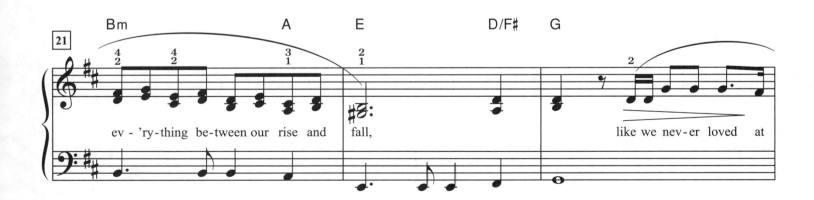

ev - 'ry-thing be-tween our rise and fall, like we nev-er loved at

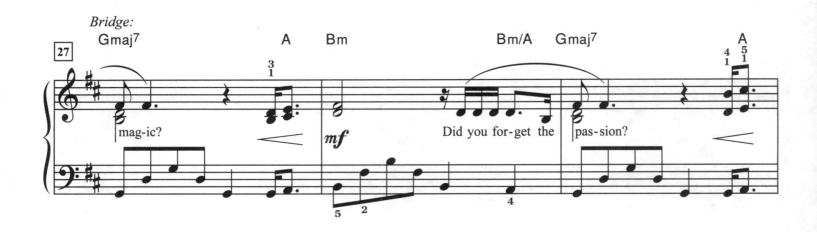

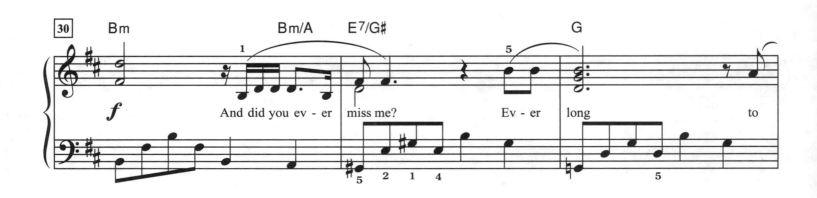

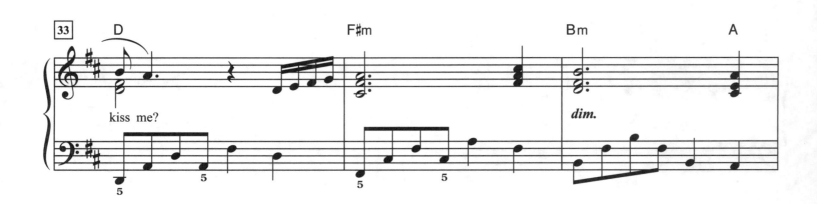

Chorus:

May-be that's just your way of deal-ing with the pain, for-get-ting

ev - 'ry-thing be-tween our rise and fall, like we nev - er loved

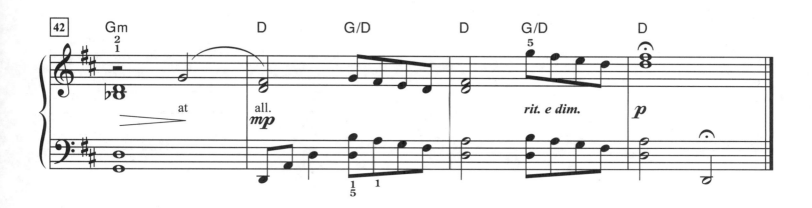

at all.

Verse 2:
You, I hear you're doing fine.
Seems like you're doing well
As far as I can tell.
Time is leaving us behind.
Another week has passed
And still I haven't laughed yet.
So tell me what your secret is
To letting go,
Letting go like you did.
How can.... *(To Chorus:)*

LIVE LIKE YOU WERE DYING

Words and Music by
Tim Nichols and Craig Wiseman
Arranged by Dan Coates

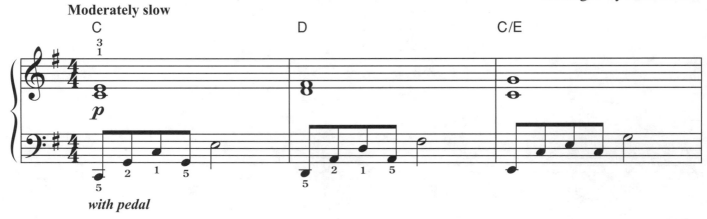

1. He said, "I was in my ear - ly for - ties___ with a
fi - nal - ly the hus - band___ that

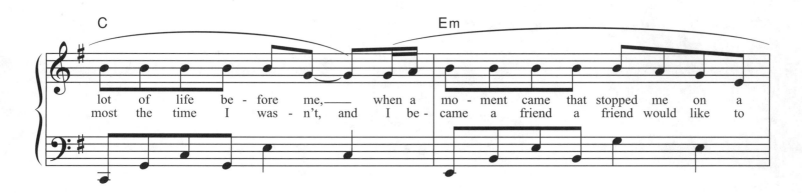

lot of life be - fore me,___ when a mo - ment came that stopped me on a
most the time I was - n't, and I be - came a friend a friend would like to

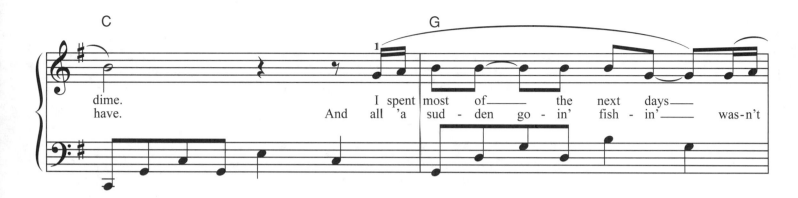

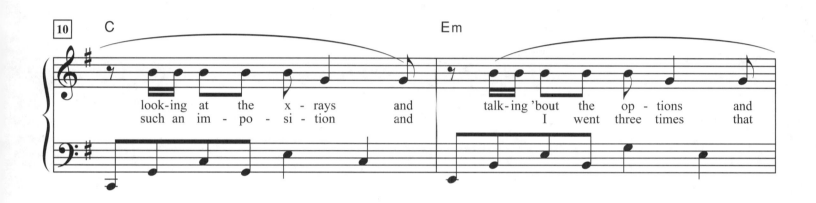

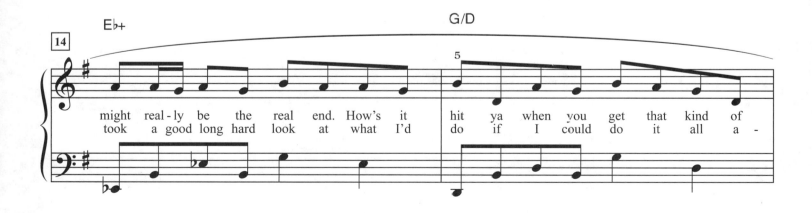

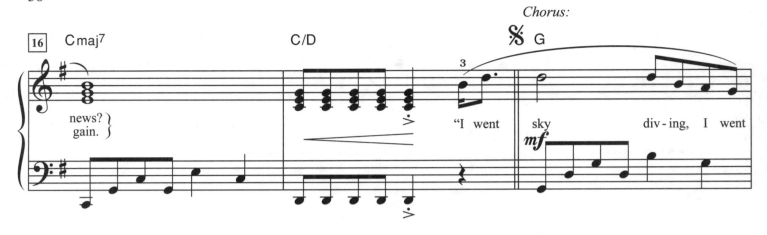

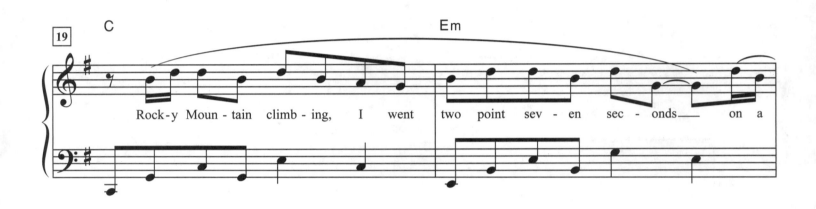

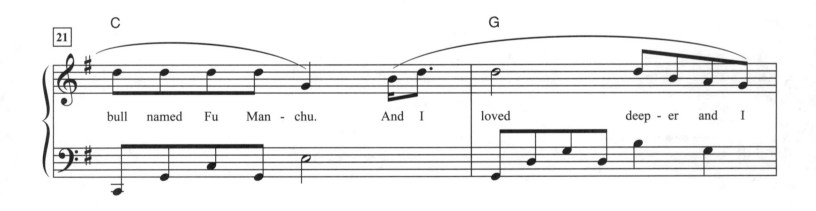

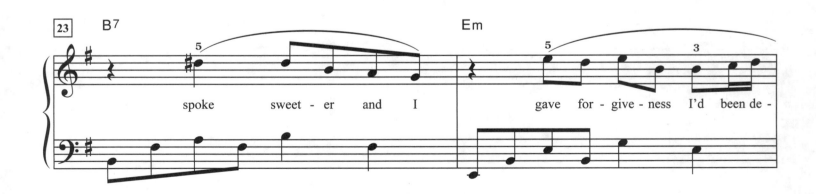

ny - ing." And he said, "Some - day I hope you get the

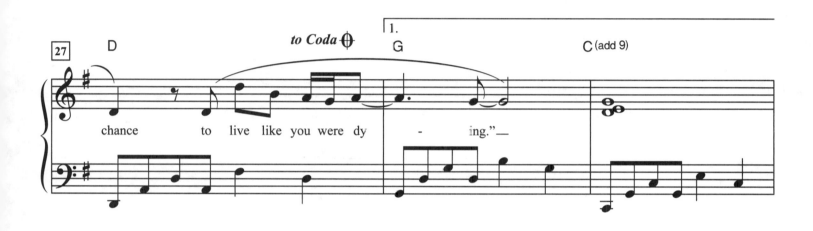

chance to live like you were dy - ing." —

He said, "I was - ing. — Like to -

Bridge:

mor - row was a gift and you've got e - ter - ni - ty to think a - bout what'd you

40

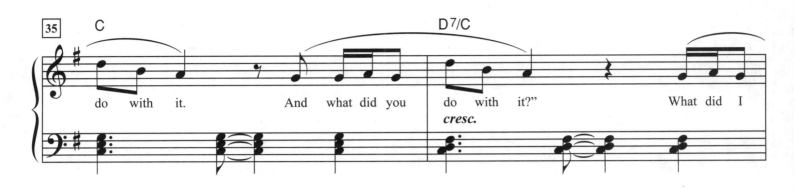

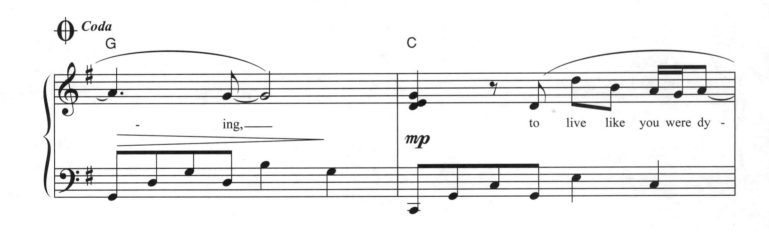

SOMETHING THAT WE DO

Words and Music by
Clint Black and Skip Ewing
Arranged by Dan Coates

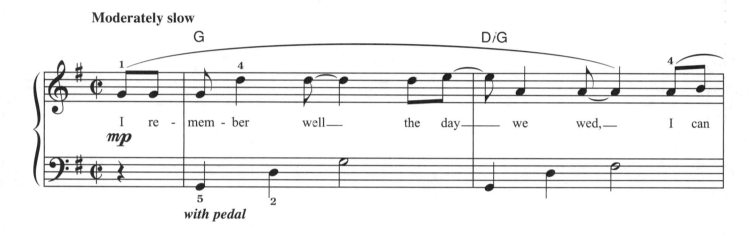

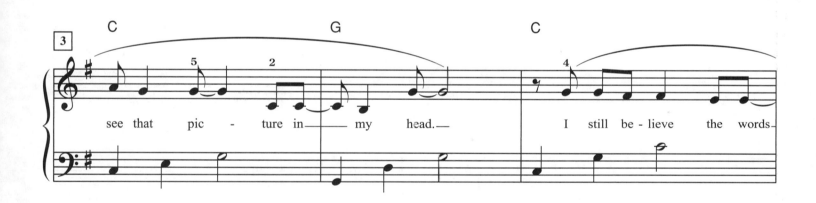

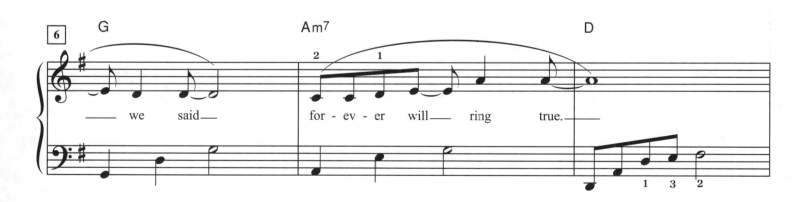

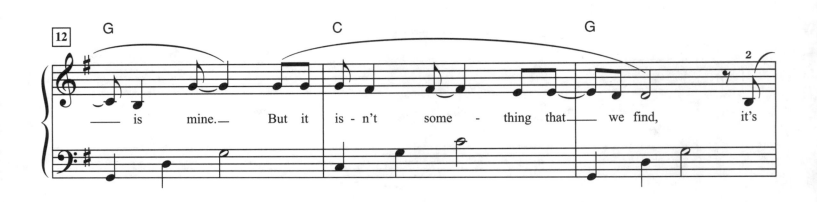

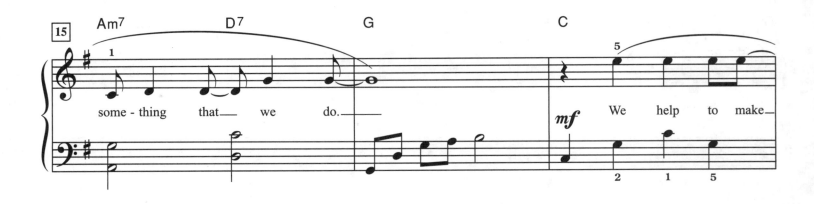

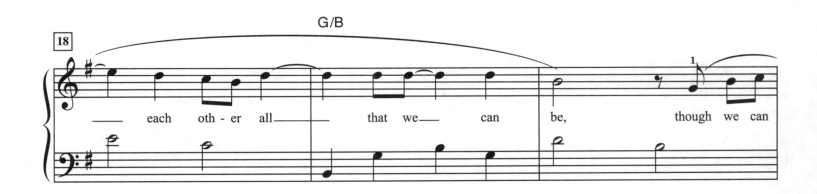

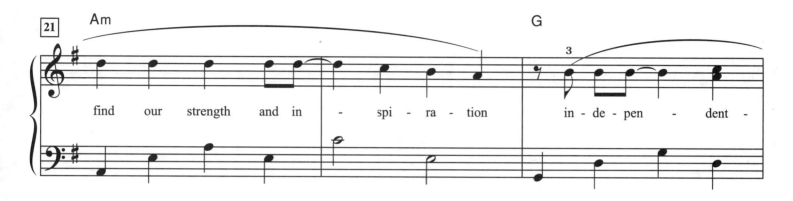

find our strength and in - spi - ra - tion   in - de - pen - dent -

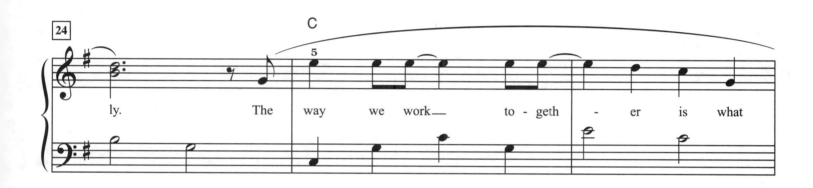

ly.   The   way   we   work   to - geth - er   is   what

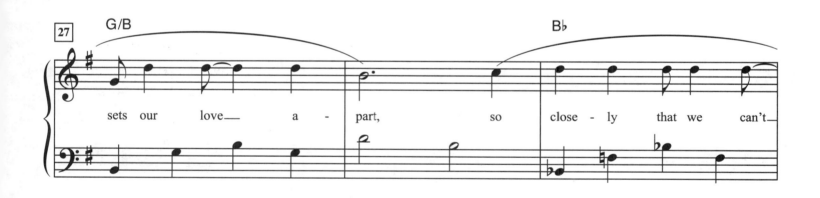

sets   our   love   a - part,   so   close - ly   that   we   can't

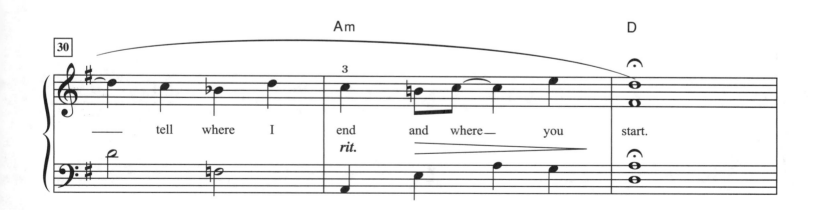

tell   where   I   end   and   where   you   start.

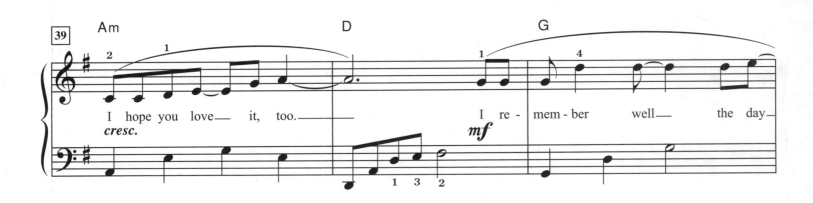

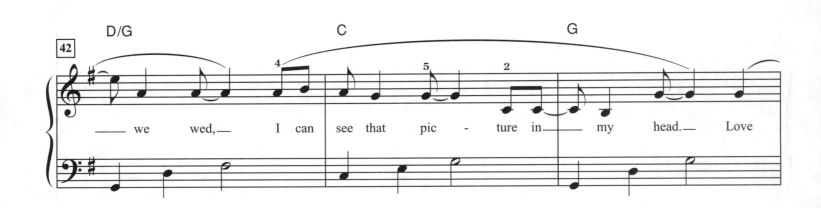

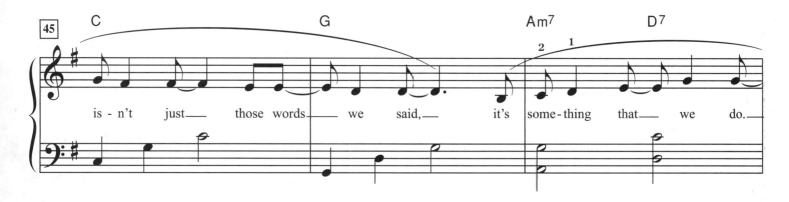

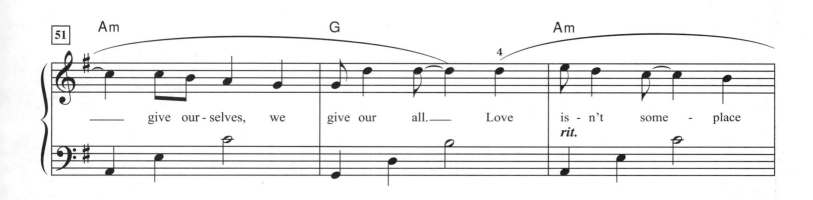

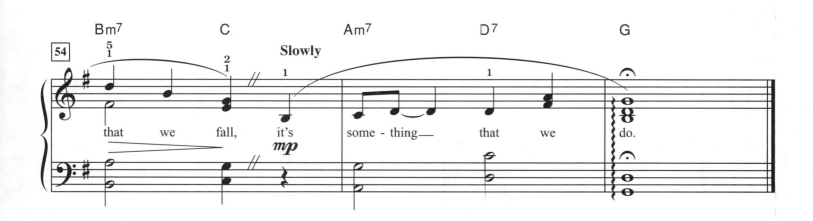

LOVE WILL ALWAYS WIN

Words and Music by
Wayne Kirkpatrick and Gordon Kennedy
Arranged by Dan Coates

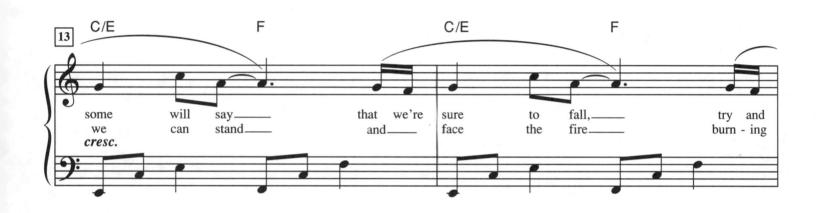

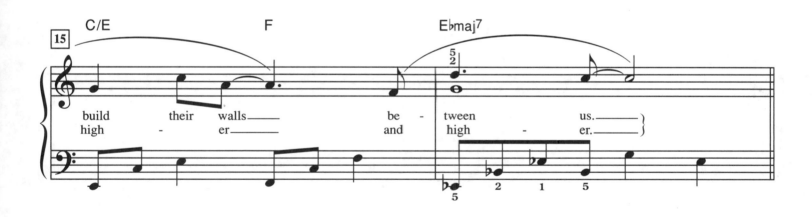

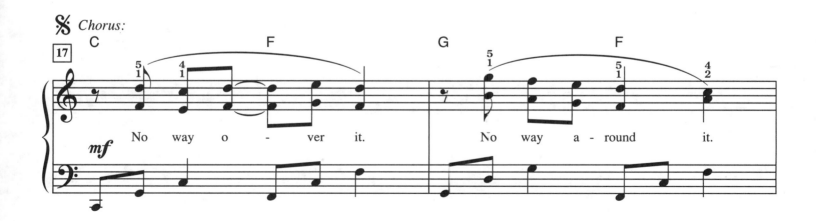

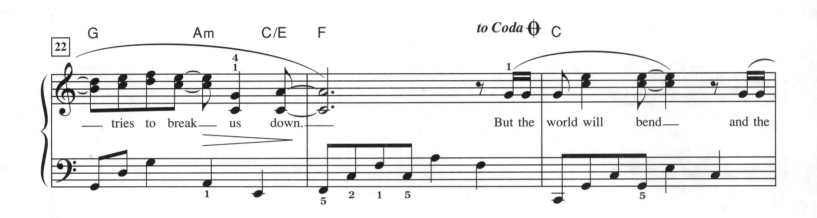

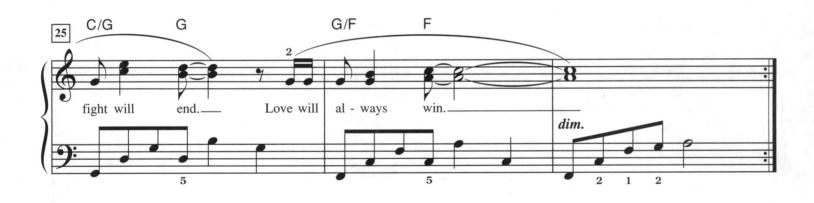

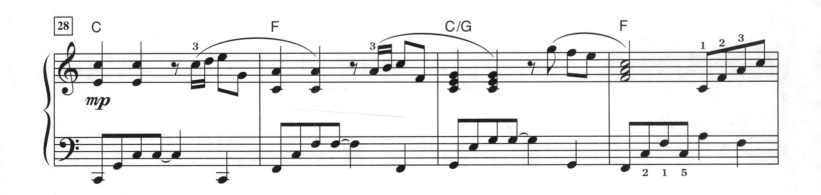

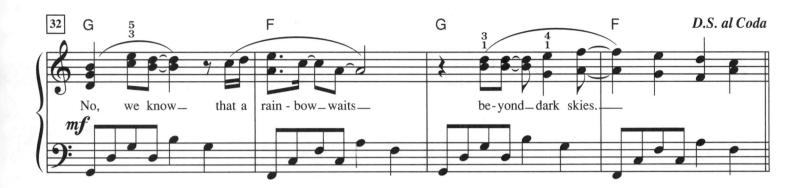

No, we know— that a rain - bow—waits— be-yond—dark skies.—

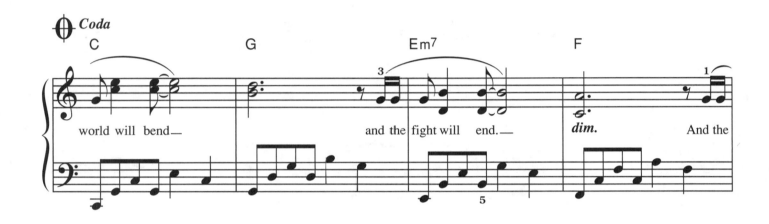

world will bend— and the fight will end.— And the

world will bend— and the fight will end.— Love will al-ways win.—

SOME HEARTS

Words and Music by
Diane Warren
Arranged by Dan Coates

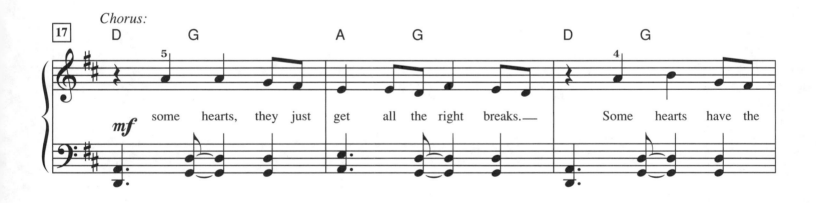

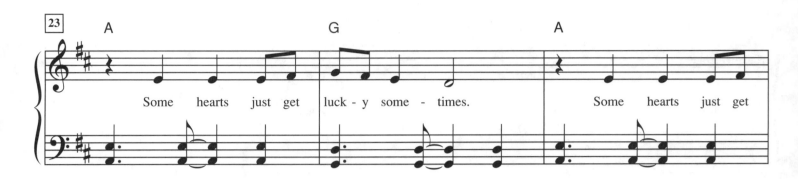

Some hearts just get luck-y some-times. Some hearts just get

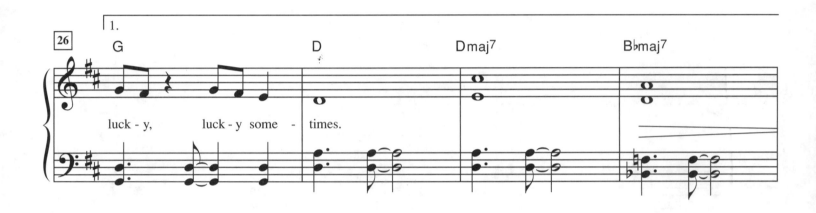

1.

luck-y, luck-y some - times.

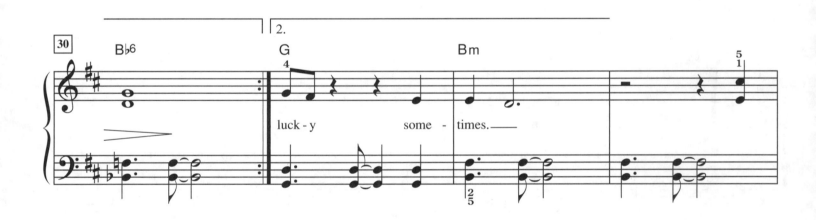

2.

luck-y some - times.——

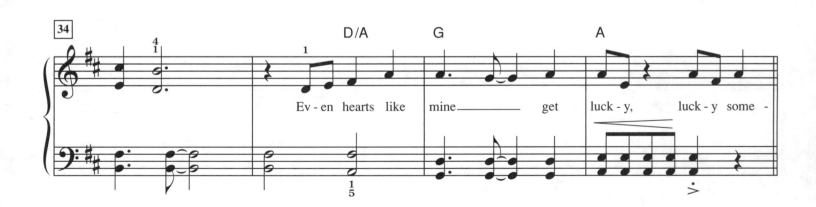

Ev - en hearts like mine—— get luck-y, luck-y some -

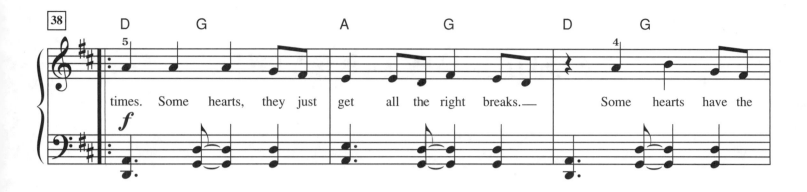

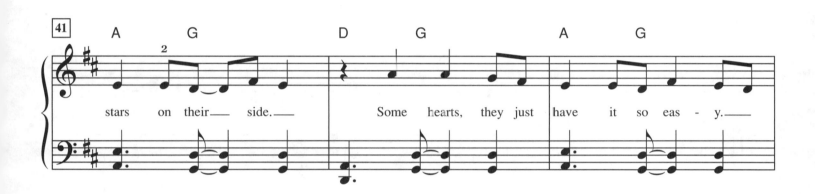

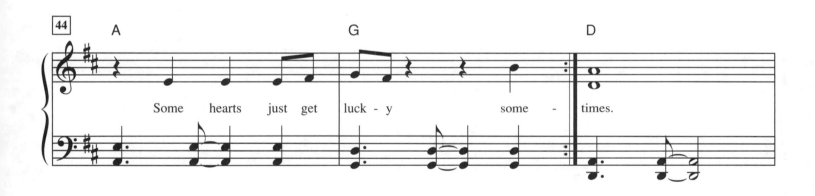

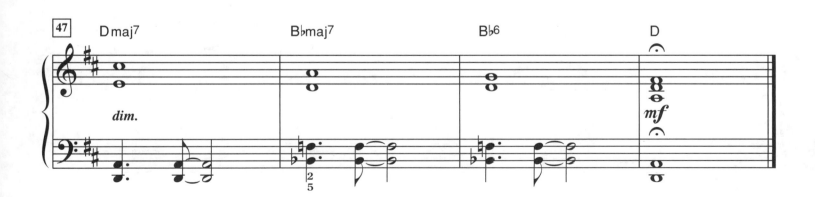

SOMEBODY LIKE YOU

Words and Music by
John Shanks and Keith Urban
Arranged by Dan Coates

1. There's a new wind blow - in' like I've
run in cir - cles, go - in'

nev - er known.— I'm breath - in' deep - er than I've
no - where fast.— I'd take one step for - ward, end up

ev - er   done.____   And it   sure   feels   good   to
two   steps   back.____   I   could - n't   walk   to   a

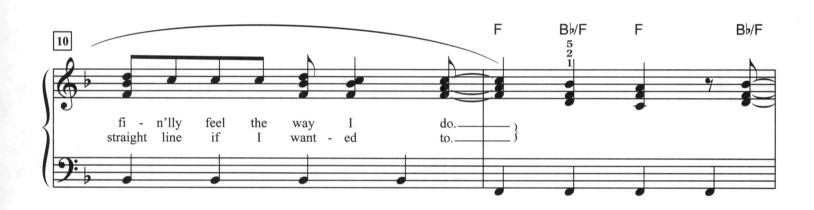

fi - n'lly   feel   the   way   I   do.____
straight   line   if   I   want - ed   to.____

Chorus:

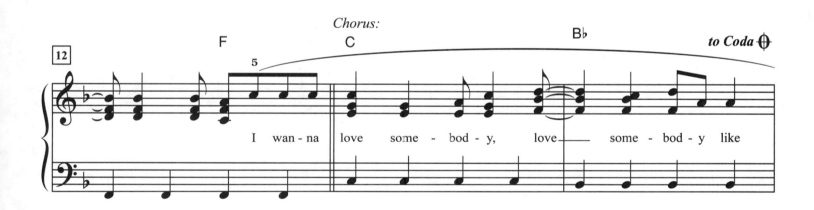

I   wan - na   love   some - bod - y,   love____   some - bod - y   like

you.   Yeah, I   wan - na   feel   sun - shine,

shin - ing down on me and you.

When you put your arms a - round me, you

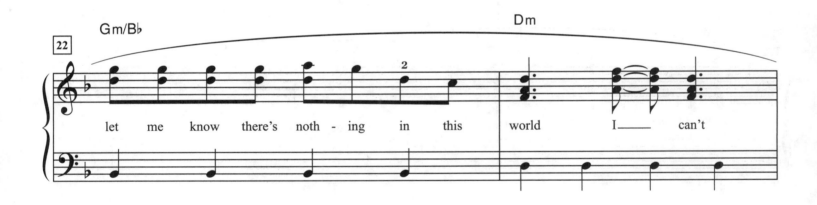

let me know there's noth - ing in this world I can't

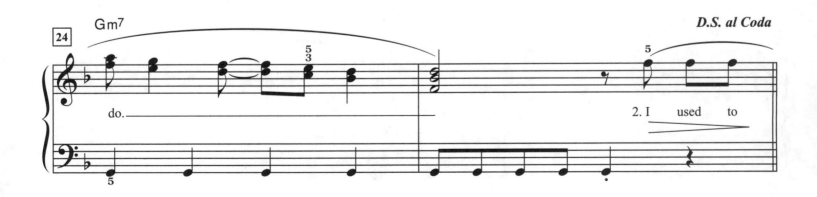

D.S. al Coda

do. 2. I used to

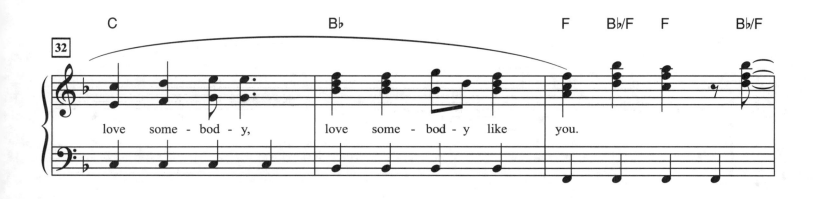

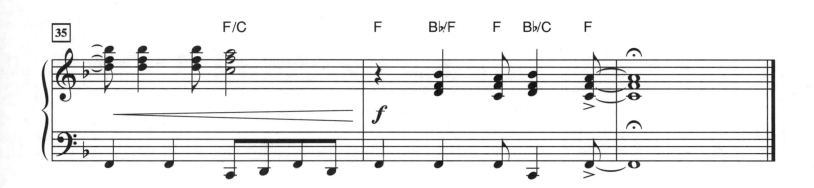

THIS KISS

Words and Music by Robin Lerner,
Annie Roboff and Beth Nielsen Chapman
Arranged by Dan Coates

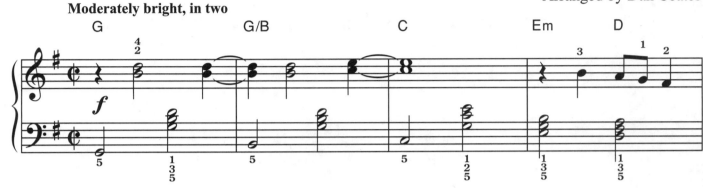

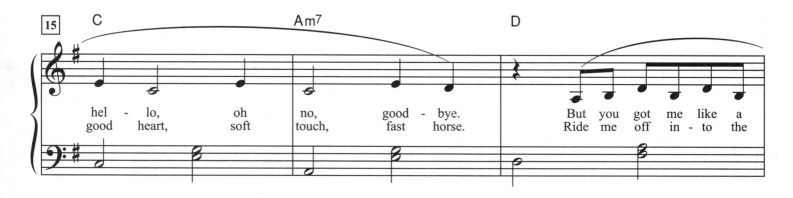

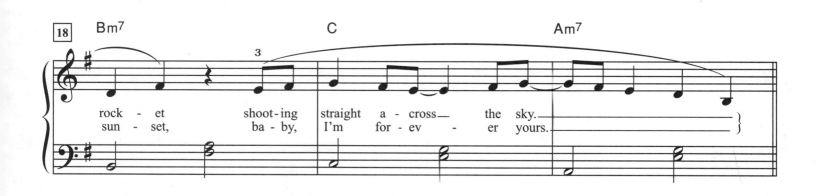

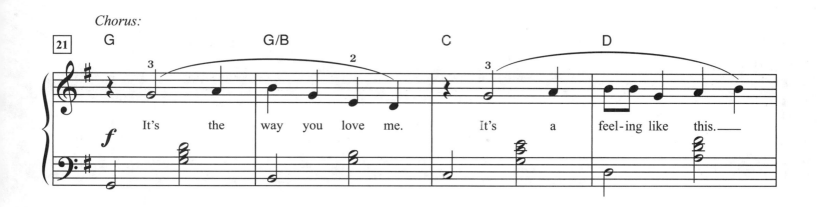

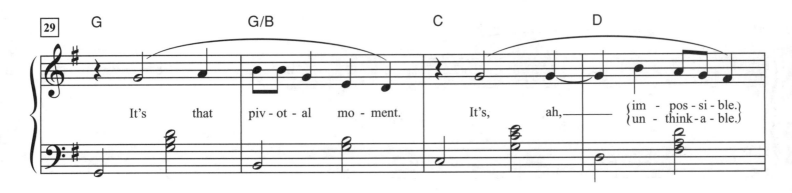

It's that piv-ot-al mo-ment. It's, ah, {im - pos - si - ble.} {un - think - a - ble.}

This kiss, this kiss, {un - stop - pa - ble.} {un - sink - a - ble.}

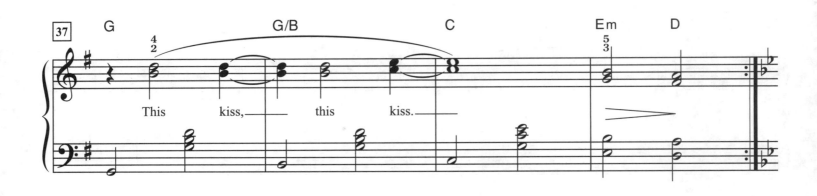

This kiss, this kiss.

Bridge:

You can kiss me in the moon - light, on the roof - top, un - der the

sky,_____ oh. You can kiss me with the win - dows o - pen while the

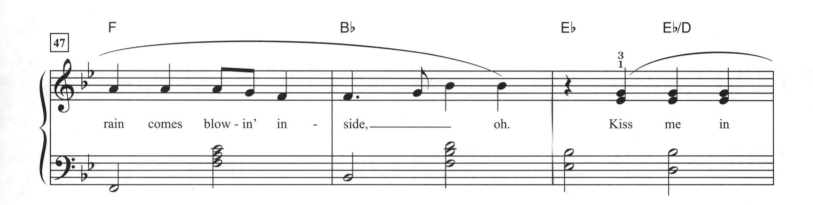

rain comes blow - in' in - side,_____ oh. Kiss me in

sweet, slow mo - tion. Let's let ev - 'ry - thing slide._____

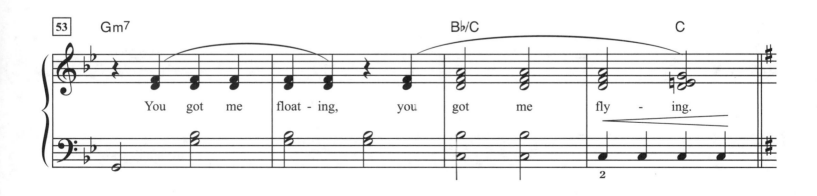

You got me float - ing, you got me fly - ing.

Chorus:

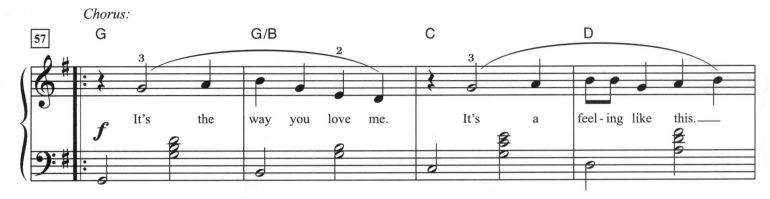

It's the way you love me. It's a feel-ing like this.___

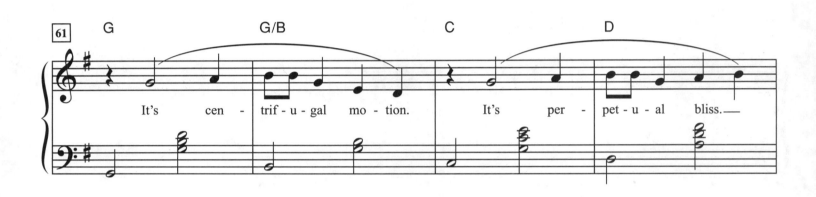

It's cen - trif - u - gal mo - tion. It's per - pet - u - al bliss.___

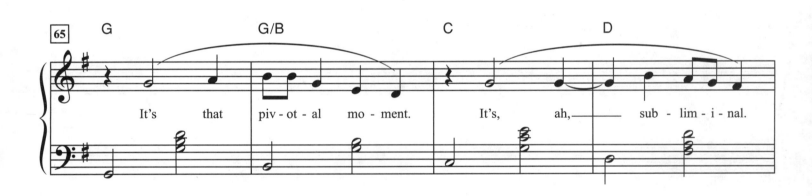

It's that piv - ot - al mo - ment. It's, ah,___ sub - lim - i - nal.

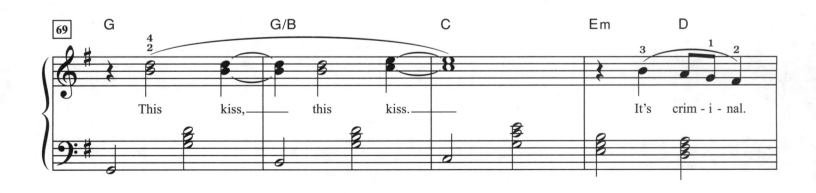

This kiss,___ this kiss.___ It's crim - i - nal.

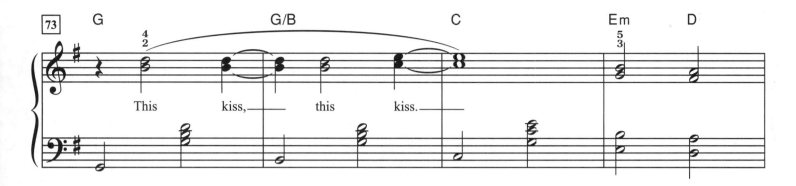

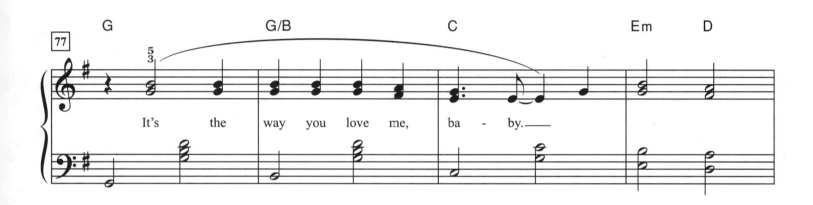

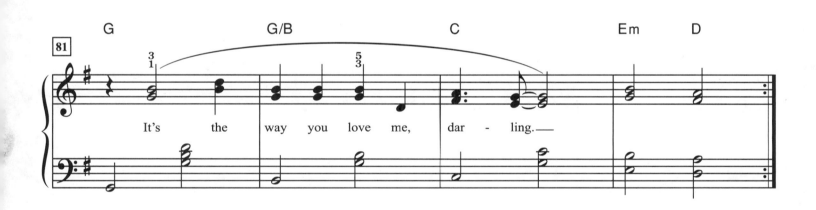

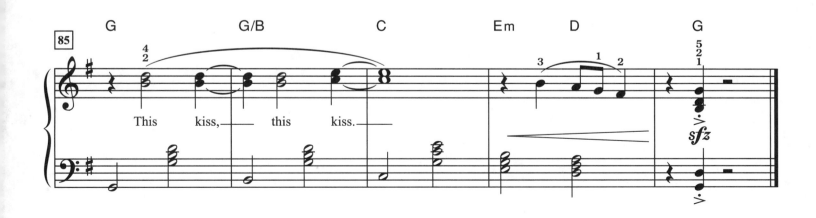